365 Days of Love

Nadine J. Wade

First edition published 2020

Dedication page

This book is dedicated to my guardian angel, my big brother Shariff Lavon Pierre Wade Aka Perry. May your soul Rest In Peace and your legacy live on forever!

The 7 Chakras

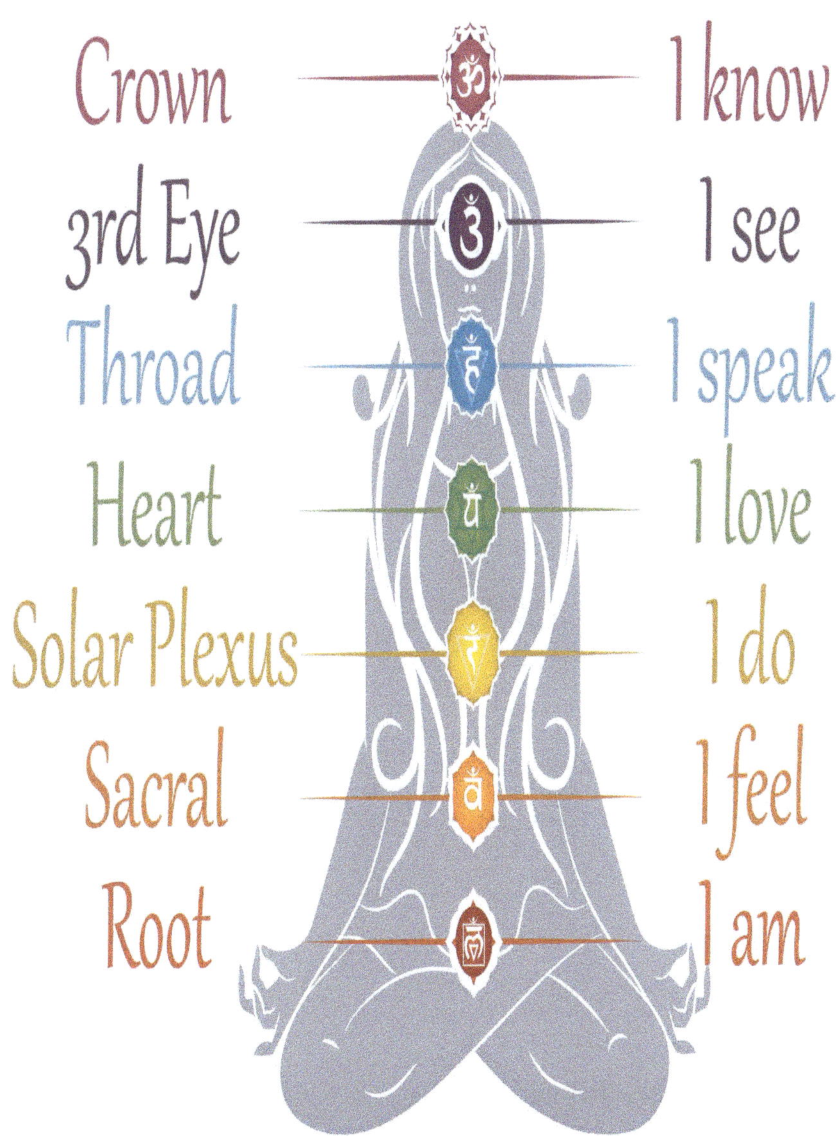

Playlist

Ribbon in the sky – Stevie Wonder

Weak- SWV

No ordinary love _ Sade

If I ever fall in love again – Boys 2 men

Twisted- Keith Sweat

My,My,My- Johnny Gill

I Swear – All 4 one

Have You Ever- Brandy

Let's get married – Jagged Edge

Whipped Cream – Ari Lennox

Ascension – Maxwell

Already Taken – Trey Songz

We don't have to take our clothes off 0 Jermaine Stewart

My Valentine – Carl Thomas

Seduce me- Celine Dion

Mirror - Justin Timberlake

When Love Calls – Atlantic starr

We found love- Rihanna

They'll never be- Switch

Summer Rain- Carl Thomas

Trip- Ella Mai

Ex –

Hold on- The internet

Not a bad thing- Justin Timberlake

Best Part – H.E.R

You – Jacquees

From Time- Drake ft Jhene Aiko

Stick With You – Pussy Cat Dolls

Rather be- Clean Bandit

Tell Me- Groove Therapy

I got A Thang- lo-key

On the run part 2- Beyoncé & Jay-z

Breathe Again- Toni Braxton

Un-break my heart- Toni Braxton

I will always love you- Whitney Houston

Its all coming back to me now – Celine Dion

Another sad love song – Toni Braxton

Red Light Special – TLC

Angel of Mine – Monica

Why I love you so much – Monica

Before you walk out of my life- Monica

Almost Doesn't Count- Brandy

Where do we go from here- Deborah Cox

One Wish- Ray J

Dear Reader,

I thank you soo much for allowing me to share my heart and mind with you. I wrote this book as an expression of love. There has been times when I was confused, rejected, and felt less than. There have been times when I poured my heart and soul into loving someone else who didn't quite love me back. Then there were times when my stomach was flustered with butterflies and I was on a beautiful love high.

This book is a reflection of my twisted love experience and how I was able to finally encounter the victory of true love. Reading this book, you too will find the answer that you've been waiting for from God. I pray that you can relate to my open, honest love stories and grow. Thank you for taking your precious time to allow me to share this love story with you.

Remember you are worth it. You are appreciated & most importantly YOU ARE ALWAYS LOVED.

-Queen Nadine J. Wade

Dear Soulmate,

First I thank the God Almighty, the Creator, and the universe for the beautiful creation of your soul. I thank your parents for giving birth to the love of my life. You are heaven sent. The universe created something special when you were conceived. Your voice is my favorite melody and music to my ears. Your eyes are the most beautiful pair of eyes I've ever seen, maybe because I get to see your beautiful soul.

Sometimes I can't even look you in the eyes because I can't believe that you are in front of me. My soul feels restored and I can't help but blush. Only God can explain the rush I get with your sweet touch. You have been nothing but the greatest friend that I could have ever asked for. There aren't enough pages in the world that could be written to describe my love for you. In your arms is my favorite place to be.

I never want to let go of your embrace. Your arms are my safe haven, my heaven, my sanctuary, my peace. Your wife, the mother of your children, the key to your heart, your favorite soul, Your goddess, your queen, your strength, your soul mate is all that I long to be. There is nothing more in this life that I want than to be your wife. Than to connect souls and create children.

You light up my life every single day. You inspire me and motivate me to become a stronger queen. Without you I am sure I would've lost my sanity. Every time I see you I get butterflies and joy fills my heart. It's a feeling that I can't get over. Waking up to you is the greatest feeling in the world. Just knowing that I am lying down next to the man of my dreams and being in your arms is my greatest escape.

You are my super hero. You deserve everything that life has to offer you. Continue to follow your dreams and never hold anything back.

Continue to stay focus on your destiny. You are surely destined for greatness. You are a beautiful strong black king. You are an angel. God gave you to this realm to bring joy, wisdom and more.

I thank you for always being there even when I am at what feels like my worse. Thank you for never going easy on me. You help to shape me in so many ways of life. Loving you has inspired me to keep going. You are the greatest friend that anyone can ever ask for. You always encourage me to do better. I have grown to know the basic principles of true love through loving you.

Every day I am working more and more on how to love myself so I can a better me. I've learned the importance of patience & to love you must be patient. I thank you for being patient with me. I learned love isn't jealous. At times I had no confidence in myself with you because I know that you deserved a strong beautiful wife. You deserved a queen and nothing less. And at times I didn't see myself as that so I'd get jealous of anyone near you.

I wondered if other woman saw the same as I did looking into your eyes or if they react the same at the sweet sound of your voice.

You are a true king. The love that I have for you will never fade away. The thought of you not in my life leaves me in tears. You radiate love and energy. I pray that your energy multiplies. Thanks for inspiring me to find my greatness and to love myself. Thank you for supporting me in times when I felt my back was against the wall.

Thanks for filling me up when I felt alone in a world full of people. Thank you for being there during my random anxiety attacks or breakdowns. Thanks for giving me the ropes to pull myself up after falling but making me pull up my own weight. Thanks for telling me off when I needed to be told about myself. Thanks for understanding me as my knowledge increased. Thank you for being who you are.

You mean the world to me. I feel like these words aren't even enough. I love you so much! I love you and wish you another prosperous day and year. I pray you become wiser today than you were yesterday. To find the greatest from within when you feel hopeless. For you to continue to grow into the king that you are. I pray for great riches and health in life. I pray for true love and true protection.

I pray that you find your purpose in life. I know that a part of my purpose is to love you. I love you and dedicate my very first book to you. So my love for you will live on forever.

-Queen Nadine J. Wade

"Love is patient,
love is kind.
It does not envy,
it does not boast,
it is not proud.
It does not dishonor others,
it is not self-seeking,
it is not easily angered,
it keeps no record of wrongs.
Love does not delight in evil but rejoices with the truth.
It always protects,
always trusts,
always hopes,
always perseveres.
Love never fails.
But where there are prophecies,
they will cease;
where there are tongues,
they will be stilled;
where there is knowledge,
it will pass away."

1 Corinthians 13:4-8

Dear King

You nurture my life like the showers bless the flowers in the spring,

only God knows the abundance of blessings you bring,

you make my heart melt like an ice sculpture in the middle of July,

when I'm with you time always seems to fly.

We don't make love because with every stroke you make it become art,

the pen to my paper, brush to my canvas, without you ...How can I start?

Before I met you my king I was heartbroken confused and shattered,

I felt like my heart was all messed up bruised and battered,

I hated red roses on Valentine's Day because that day, that day felt like a funeral

I was so scared because I knew what the wrong love could do to you.

Then one day I picked my head up high.

I saw the angels and God cleared the grey stormy skies.

The ice sculpture around my heart melted and I felt brand new.

I learned to love myself so that I could be the Queen to love you.

To love you king the way you should be loved,

Because I know that you would turn out to be just the type of guy I'd been thinking of.

See, I can tell you all the things I know you'd do,

The only problem is .... I still haven't found you.

I know when I do, like Cinderella the shoe will surely fit.

I'd look you deep in your eyes with bliss and joyful tears and say "this is it"

I found you King.

You are surely the one.

You will kiss my heart like the oceans waves and the sun,

and every time I see you my heart wouldn't help but skip a beat.

God will smile upon us at his great defeat.

No weapon formed against us will prosper.

Not even if you were Muslim, Jew or Rasta.

Our energies will hold a bond so strong that not even we could explain.

You'd be my superman and I your Lois lane.

I know you're out there calling for me too.

Just know that your queen is here waiting for you.

What is love?

Brittany: "Love is life. Love is energy. Love is the universe."

Do you believe in love at first sight?

Brittany: "Yes I believe in love at first sight. It's an automatic connection. It's more so physical, mental connection. You know?"

Love is selfless.

1+1

2 people but my love for you makes me feel like we're connected as 1.

You are a part of me so there is nothing I can't overcome.

When I lose sight you help me see.

I never feel alone in life because your love has been instilled within me,

Just the sound of your voice makes my walls crumble.

The look in your eyes makes my heart rumble and the slightest touch drives me insane and sends chills to some places and the sweetest thoughts rush to my brain.

1+1 =2

but there is no me without you.

In a relationship

"In a relationship you need somebody who's going to call you out, not somebody who's going to let everything slide.

You need somebody who doesn't want to live without you but can.

Not somebody that is dependent, but somebody who is stronger with you.

A relationship is two people not one."

My light

You light up my life.

You make my eyes sparkle and heart skip a beat.

You, my love, sweep me off of my feet.

When I see you at times, I forget to breathe in air, only because the man of my dreams is so close and near.

You are the light of my life,

I'd do whatever just to hear you speak.

You leave me so vulnerable and weak.

Your existence alone inspires me and puts me in another zone.

I can do anything with the thought of loving you alone.

You are the light at the end of any tunnel that I may go through.

You light up my life and I love you.

Love is patient.

Fun Fact: Female elephants might give birth every five years, and continue to mate until about the age of 50. The female elephant's pregnancy will last up to 23 months, longer than many other animals. On average, newborn calves stand about 9 m (3 ft.) high and weigh 120 kg (264 lb.) at birth. Newborn male African elephants may weigh up to 165 kg (364 lb.).

Elephants represent patience to me. Not everything in life will come easy. Some things you must take time to grow so that in due time the world will feel the arrival of your time. Be patient with yourself and with love. In time you will find the one for you.

11:11

11:11 make a wish

I closed my eyes and felt your lips

In your arms head on your chest

When I laid my soul to rest

Your heart then began to race

Everything was all in place

Our souls began to tie

Nothing mattered but you and I

In that moment we were one

Like God did the moon and sun

Our love deeper than the ocean

The universe had put our love in motion

11:11 made my wish

You and I in full bliss

God's plan

My purpose in life is surely to love you

To take your cloudy days and turn them a sunny blue

To smile at you and look into your eyes

To hold you tight as time swiftly flies

To make you laugh even while you are in pain

To carry your children and to keep your last name

My soul purpose in life is to unconditionally love you

Love Vs Lust

Sometime we get so caught up in this magical feeling of love that we mistake love for lust.

The difference between Love and Lust

Love	Lust
Love is patient	Lust is from the world
Love is selfless	Lust you must have it now
Love is giving	Lust is selfish
Love is purity	Lust is sin
Love develops	Lust destroys
Love is peaceful	Lust creates anxiety

Love Word Search

Love Word Search

1 Corinthians 13:4-8

Find the hidden words.

K Y D S N G E G I P B E E E H
U P A E M L G A A V E A B O N
W R T V Q F P R R J A T P W E
U E I E Z J R B R Z R E O P Z
U N R I G H T E O U S N E S S
N E B L B Q P P G F M H C J K
N S Q E K E R S A V P P R P X
E J E B C O P T N C M L C X Q
R N S C V O N E T N X J J T C
D P D O I E M D E R E F F U S
Y N K U I O R I J E A L O U S
R E I T R D J O N F L C G V K
D R A K F E Z E A G X M K O F
Z P Y Z D A S R R R L S R A W
Q T K X B W R E V E N Y Y C N

Is **PATIENT**

Is **KIND**

Is Not **JEALOUS**

Does Not **BRAG**

Is Not **ARROGANT**

Does Not Act **UNBECOMINGLY**

Does Not Seek Its **OWN**

Is Not **PROVOKED**

Does Not Take Into Account A Wrong **SUFFERED**

Does Not Rejoice In **UNRIGHTEOUSNESS**

REJOICES With The Truth

BEARS All Things

BELIEVES All Things

HOPES All Things

ENDURES All Things

The Heartbreak

There was a thick silence,

every vessel in my body had been replaced by chills.

Who knew that love had the power to kill.

Heavy tears rushed down my cheeks.

Stomach cringed like I hadn't eaten for weeks.

My heart became silent no more pulsating.

The air was thin and in that moment I realized that it had been true love.

I gasped for air but my throat closed,

I couldn't breathe.

That was a vision I just couldn't believe.

I became numb, frozen and my body was still.

There I laid as I became a corpse.

The Illusion

I love you.

When I say it I mean it.

I'll give you all the love in my heart I've already asked God to clean it.

I let everyone go so you are all I have.

And I want you to be my better half.

I can't do this alone because it's all about us building a strong foundation.

I just ask you to be my king and the ruler of my nation.

To be the one to build a dynasty with me based on our design,

influenced by God, touched with a lil bit of yours and mine.

I want to put you on a pedestal and treat you like a king.

I promise you, joy is all I want to bring.

I desire to put a smile on your face everyday

But you push me away,

telling me that I should wait for a future that doesn't seem too clear

because one minute you'er here the next you're there.

I pray for you but your actions sometimes point me to you not being the one.

Your actions say this is all to you just for fun.

Truth is I'll never wake up to you everyday and hold you at night.

This relationship will reach higher than this height.

I did have doubt before but then I thought,

what if we are meant to be

What if you are the one God has sent for me?

If so why are your actions so iffy.

But then I have hope again when you lean in to kiss me.

Maybe that's just the devil trying to fill my mind with doubt.

I miss you so much right now it's hard to figure it out.

Pushing Apart

You push, I push

We can't keep pushing each other away.

All I know is that tomorrow isn't guaranteed another day.

I might not have a chance to say I love you or hear your voice.

To love you is all that I want to do, I've made my choice

I push, you push,

Let's push to unite.

Us not speaking just isn't right.

Whatever it is we can work it out.

We can move forward even if we might have to reroute.

I can't go too long without my homie, lover and best friend.

Anything wrong, love can surely mend

5 Love Languages

How to relate to a person with this love language...	COMMUNICATION	ACTION	WHAT TO AVOID
Words of Affirmation	Compliments Affirmations Kind words	Send notes or cards.	Criticism
Quality Time	One-on-one time. Not interrupting. Face-to-face conversation.	Take long walks together. Do things together. Take trips.	Long periods of being apart. More time with friends than with partner.
Receiving Gifts	Positive, fact-oriented information.	Give gifts on special occasions and also on not so special occasions.	Forgetting special days.
Acts of Service	Action words like "I can," "I will," "What else can I do?"	Helping with house and yard chores. Repair/maintenance. Acts of kindness.	Ignoring partner's requests while helping others.
Physical Touch	A lot of non-verbal. Verbal needs to be "word pictures".	Touches Hugs Pats Kisses	Physical neglect or abuse.

Sleepless Nights

Another cold sleepless night of tossing and turning mixed with over thinking a small argument.

Tears quietly rush down my face.

I grab the pillow closely and tight imagining I was holding him.

Thoughts cloud my head as I look at my phone to see missed calls and none from him.

Could this be the end of us?

Does he not love me after all?

He was never your "boyfriend" anyway so why do you feel this way?

Look at you? You don't even deserve him and can't do anything right!

I pick myself up the next morning eyes swollen from the tears the night before.

The sun seems too bright and nothing seems to faze me.

No appetite to eat the cold breakfast that my roommate made me to cheer me up earlier before work.

I couldn't eat anything all day forcing myself to fast in my own depression.

Alexa play Whipped Cream Ari Lennox.

Music plays.

Those nights

I miss the nights that I found hard to resist.

The nights when I was craving more than your kiss.

When we talk for hours always finding something to say.

I'd Blush at the conversation we had the next day.

I missed when I love you meant I never want to be the reason you cry.

And I miss you meant I'd give it a try.

Try anything just to see your face.

Anything just to feel your warm embrace.

Those nights that I would never forget.

Not even the nights I wish I could press reset.

Hope is the only thing stronger than fear.

The happiness subsided and pain keeps replaying in my mind. This can't be love I outta be blind.

I Can Hope

I can write you a poem or even a song
Hoping you'll fall in love or sing along
I can shower you with love and gifts
Hoping that one day your heart starts to shift
I can show you how much I truly love and care
Hoping that one day I'll wake up and you'll be there
I can pray for you, like I do
Hoping that one day my love will find you
I can lift you up when you are feeling down
Hoping that one day you'll notice my crown
I can forgive you and treat you well
Hoping that God reveals what only He can tell
I can make your favorite meal so you can eat
Hoping that it'll sweep you off your feet
I can be patient and wait on the lord
Hoping to receive the same love that I've poured
I can hold my head high and stand tall
Hoping that one, it'll be worth the fall

Trust Issues

Trust is the relationship.

If there is no trust then there is no relationship.

If we have issues, we must look internally and solve them from introspect and self-awareness.

Trust always starts with your view and your ability to hold yourself up when the situation wants you to drown.

Do not allow insecurity and fear of the past to block your ability to trust now.

You cannot afford to waste any more time doing that.

Trust is the ticker to the freedom that you need.

To be trusted is a compliment greater than to be loved.

What is yours will find you no matter what.

You are enough.

Queen

That's my name, can never be worn out
The only creation that'll come up with water in a drought
I'm everything in between love and respect
When I look in the mirror I smile at the image I reflect
It's in the way that I walk, talk and how God crafted my crown
How much higher I rise up if ever I fall down
The beauty in my smile, style and grace
In competition with no one, running my own race
Queen
When that sun hits me, my skin resembles gold
Rich in my roots, can never be sold
My mind like magic will leave you in awe
Perfect beauty from the naked eye to my core
A wombman, the one that gives life

This page is meant for you to just write how you feel inside about something that might be troubling your spirit. Let it all out here!

____

____

____

____

____

____

____

____

____

____

Now that you got that off of your chest. Try these affirmations for 7 days straight.

I am loved

I am blessed

I am healing

I am strong

I am capable

I am amazing

I am royalty

Dear Beautiful Soul,

I just want you to know that the journey of love isn't always sweet and easy. However love itself is what we were created to do. God is love. Love is patient, love is kind,.....

It is important to know the difference between love and lust. It is important to recognize the true signs of true love. Don't forget to pray for guidance and complete answers. Do not rush love its best that you take time. Instead of running into relationship after relationship, learn to simply love yourself. Self love is vital to any relationship.

We must learn to love ourselves and the only way we can truly learn to love ourselves is to know how God loves us. When you love yourself you get to know yourself and you are able to truly know what it is that you would want in a relationship. It's very important that we know our love language and our partners as well so that way we are able to build strong healthy loving understanding relationships.

I've been denied love before. I've been the one over loving someone who didn't love me back. I was looking crazy however I was blind. I didn't see that God didn't want me with that person. In fact he had bigger, better plans for my life. So I just say this to you out there feeling inadequate, you are enough. You are perfect. You were created in his image and his likeness. Don't let anyone make you feel less than that. Love yourself! God knows the desires of your heart. It is up to you to make the decision of what next you will do with it.

Go out there and find yourself. Explore the world and try new things. Get to know who you are. Don't settle for anything less than what

God has set for you. The journey of self love isn't always easy but it's most important after God's love. Now that you know a little more about Gods love look forward to my new book 365 days of Self love. I love you. God bless you, take care. Remember God is love.

Yours truly

-Queen Nadine .J. Wade

About the Author

- Nadine Wade is a New York Times best selling author, entrepreneur, influencer from the Bronx New York. She influences people across multiple disciplines globally to love themselves and follow their dreams. She enjoys giving back to her community and inspiring people through all platforms. She is well known for her YouTube channel Ask Queen Nadine, dancing and her high class cleaning service. She enjoys traveling and connecting with great people. The love for God and her family is the fuel to her success. Nadine uses writing as one of her greatest expressions of her heart. 365 days of love is her first published work of art. She gives thanks to her mother Miss Ledria Simone Wade for her limitless creative mind and unconditional love. She wants you to know that All things are possible through Christ and you must first believe. Contact her at *asknadiine@gmail.com*

www.ingramcontent.com/pod-product-compliance
Ingram Content Group UK Ltd.
Pitfield, Milton Keynes, MK11 3LW, UK
UKHW021828270726
14058UKWH00001B/39

9 781716 081811